# HARDIK PANDYA COLOUR

INDIAN CRICKETER

MR VIVEK KUMAR PANDEY SHAMBHUNATH

ISBN 979-888530678-2

Short biography of Hardik Pandya and about life.During writing this book no character & no religious are harmed written by Mr Vivek Kumar Pandey. winner youngest writer award 1st rank in india 2020.He is only one writer can publish 700+ own book that was greatest successfull in his life . This book fully colour edition books.

# Contents

# Foreword

**Author biography in English** :MY NAME IS VIVEK KUMAR PANDEY . I WAS BORN IN 30 SEP 2002,I AM FROM SURAT GUJARAT INDIA.MY DREAM WAS TO BE GOOD WRITERS ,MY FAMILY SUPPORTED ME TO SUCCESSFUL AND I CAN DO IT MY SELF.How do I write? That is a question, I believe, that cannot be honestly answered by me."CELEBRATING YOUNGEST WRITER AWARD WINNER IN GUJARAT 1ST RANK" MR PANDEY JI . I may think I did a good job writing something when in reality it could be horrible. The reader is the one who decides the quality of my writing. I do not find writing to be natural to me and therefore find it to be a real challenge. My trick as a challenged writer is to do the best I can and know that I am happy with the final outcome. It may take a while to do my best and there may be quite a few problems I run into along the way.

I am not a greedy person those who are thinking about me and my self I never tried it anyone people suffering from sadness ,I trying to get promoted people suffering from happiness and joy in your Life Time. Now in current situation in India and also world people are unemployed and have no many but our indian governor help to people to get free food from ration card , i also take part in leadership team ,i am Motivational speaker , Film script writer. There was my two dream firstly writer and secondly actor & also my own film is upcoming soon i done almost completely completed script for my film .I AM GOING TO SAY WORD OF HEART TOUCH OUT PLEASE READ IT" , firstly i thanks my father he supports me in this field they always getting inspired me by own his words and behavior ,they always said that he was a biggest person in the world in future and also they purchase fruit and chocolate for me in anytime & anyway , firstly my father buy him then call me Vivek you want a chocolate i will say yes papa but how many tell me ,papa: you tell me how much i buy him i told 1 or 2 chocolate but my father purchase whole the boxes of chocolate and they get suprised me. MY FATHER WAS BORN IN " 20 SEPTEMBER" 1971 IN INDIA.

1) MY FATHER FAVORITE CLOTHES IS KURTA PAIJMA AND ALSO STYLES SHOE

2) FAVORITE SINGER IS KISHORE DA

3) FAVORITE STATE GUJARAT AND KOLKATA , HIS VILLAGE IN BIHAR

4) FAVORITE COLOR BLACK AND WHITE

THEY ALSO LOVE cricket like IPL and one day t-20 .they also like watching a News daily and heard the song daily ,they also interested in tik tok video but in current time tik tok is banned in india but also few videos are in you tube. In lockdown time my family and me very enjoy day daily. my father play daily ludo with his sister and son, daughter.they always loved tea and coffee anytime call me "। विवेक थोड़ा चाय बनाओना विवेक तुम्हारे हाथ का चाय अच्छा लगता है". I make it tea for my father but some reason after the April to june they are suffering from fever and cough , weakness on 6 June 2020 my father death. they not told me say bye bye his life. After death of 6 June on 10 june my mom and dad anniversary.but my father is Best in the world they can do anything for me please take care of father and respect it of your parents.

CHAPTER ONE

# Hardik Pandya Colour

- *Hardik Pandya*

Hardik Himanshu Pandya (born 11 October 1993) is an Indian international cricketer who plays for Baroda in domestic cricket and Mumbai Indians in the Indian Premier League (IPL). He is an all-rounder who bats right-handed and bowls right-arm fast-medium. His elder brother Krunal Pandya is also an international cricketer.

1. Early years

Hardik Pandya was born on 11 October 1993 in Surat, Gujarat. His father Himanshu Pandya, ran a small car finance business in Surat which he shut down and shifted to Vadodara when Hardik was five; he did so in order to facilitate his sons with better cricket training facilities. He enrolled his two sons (Hardik and Krunal) into Kiran More's cricket academy in Vadodara.Financially weak, the Pandya family lived in a rented apartment in Gorwa, with the brothers using a second-hand car to travel to the cricket ground. Hardik studied at the MK High School until ninth grade before dropping out to focus on cricket.

Hardik made steady progress in junior-level cricket and, according to Krunal, "won a lot of matches single-handedly" in club cricket. In an interview with the Indian Express, Hardik revealed that he was dropped from his state age-group teams due to his "attitude problems." He added that he was "just an expressive child" who does not "like to hide his emotions."

According to his father, Hardik was a leg spinner until the age of 18 and turned to fast bowling at the insistence of the Baroda coach Sanath Kumar.

- *Domestic career*

Pandya has been playing for Baroda cricket team since 2013. He played a vital role in Baroda winning the Syed Mushtaq Ali Trophy in the 2013–14 season. In January 2016, he slammed eight sixes during his innings unbeaten 86 to guide Baroda cricket team to a six-wicket win over Vidarbha cricket team in the Syed Mushtaq Ali Trophy.

- Indian Premier League

Pandya plays for Mumbai Indians in the Indian Premier League. Against Kolkata Knight Riders, in a must-win situation for Mumbai Indians to remain in the race for the top 4 teams, he scored a quickfire 61 off 31 balls to win the match for his side and earn his second man of the match award in the season. He was also awarded the 'Yes Bank maximum sixes award' for the same match.

- *International career*

- T20Is

Pandya made his Twenty20 International debut for India on 27 January 2016 at the age of 22, picking up 2 wickets against Australia. His first Twenty20 International wicket was Chris Lynn. In the second T20I against Sri Lanka cricket team at Ranchi, he batted ahead of Yuvraj Singh and MS Dhoni and hit 27 off 14 balls before becoming hat-trick victim of Thisara Perera.

In Asia Cup 2016, Pandya smashed an 18-ball 31 helping India post a respectable score against Bangladesh. Later on, he also picked up a wicket to secure the win. In the next match against Pakistan he bowled his best figures of 3 for 8 which restricted Pakistan to 83. In a 2016 World Twenty20 match against Bangladesh on 23 March, Pandya took two crucial wickets in the last three balls of match's final over as India beat Bangladesh by one run. His career best bowling figures of 4 for 38 was achieved in the 3rd and final Twenty20 International against England on 8 July 2018, he got 33 Not Out in 14 balls, hitting the winning runs with a six off Jordan. Hardik became first Indian to take 4 wickets and score above 30 runs in a T20I in the same match.

In September 2021, Pandya was named in India's squad for the 2021 ICC Men's T20 World Cup.

- *ODI career*

Pandya made his One Day International (ODI) debut for India against New Zealand on 16 October 2016 at Dharamshala. He became the fourth Indian to be named player of the match on ODI debut after Sandeep Patil, Mohit Sharma and K. L. Rahul. In his first ODI innings as a batsman, he scored 36 runs from 32 balls. In the group stages of ICC Champions Trophy, Pandya hit three consecutive sixes off Imad Wasim in the same over before rain stopped play. On 18 June 2017, in the final of the Champions Trophy at the Oval, he struck a 43-ball 76 in a losing cause, after coming in with India at 54/5 following a top order collapse.

He was selected in the ODI XI of the year 2017.

In April 2019, he was named in India's squad for the 2019 Cricket World Cup.On 27 June 2019, in the match against the West Indies, Pandya played in his 50th ODI.

- *Test career*

Pandya was included in India's Test squad for their home series against England in late 2016, but was eventually left out after he injured himself while training in the nets at the PCA Stadium. He was named in the squad that toured Sri Lanka in July 2017 and played his first Test on 26 July in Galle. In the 3$^{rd}$ and the final Test match against Sri Lanka at Pallekele, Pandya scored his maiden Test century, and set the record for becoming the first Indian batsman to score a Test century just before lunch. He also set the record for scoring the most runs in a single over of a Test innings for India, scoring 26 runs.This century was his first century in international cricket.

- *Personal life*

Pandya got engaged to an Indian-based Serbian dancer and actress Nataša Stanković on 1 January 2020. On 30 July, their first child, Agastya Pandya, was born.

Pandya with brother Krunal during Mumbai Indians‘ victory celebration after 2017 Indian Premier League

His brother Krunal Pandya has also played for India and the Mumbai Indians. Their father, Himanshu Pandya passed away on January 2021, following a cardiac arrest.

- *Controversy*

In January 2019, Pandya appeared with teammate K. L. Rahul on the show Koffee with Karan, and made several controversial comments which were met with immediate public backlash. During the interview, Pandya spoke about how he had proudly informed his parents of his first sexual encounter, which was well received by them. He also proclaimed that he likes to "observe how women move" at high-end bars and nightclubs, as well as on social media and then went on to liken himself to a black person saying, "I'm a little from the black side so I need to see how they move". The public categorized his monologue as indecent, derogatory, misogynistic and disgraceful. Pandya apologized for his remarks by saying that he had gotten carried away by the nature of the show.

The Board of Control for Cricket in India (BCCI) responded to the controversy by saying, "It will be considered whether players should even be allowed to appear on such shows which have got nothing to do with cricket.

" The BCCI found the comments as very crass, sexist and cringeworthy,and was not impressed by the apology, seeking appropriate legal action into the matter as it was a breach of conduct.Both Pandya and Rahul were handed a suspension until a pending investigation and were called back from the ongoing tours of Australia and New Zealand. Furthermore, on 13 January 2019, Gillette suspended their brand association with Pandya for its Mach3 razor. On 24 January 2019, after lifting the suspension on Pandya and Rahul, the BCCI announced that Pandya would re-join the squad for the matches in New Zealand.

- *2016 Asia Cup Squad*

The 2016 Asia Cup (also called the Micromax Asia Cup T20) was a Twenty20 International (T20I) cricket tournament that was held in Bangladesh from 24 February to 6 March 2016. It was the $13^{th}$ edition of the Asia Cup, the fifth to be held in Bangladesh, and the first to be played using the T20I format. Bangladesh hosted the tournament for the third consecutive time after 2012 and 2014. Micromax was the main sponsor of the tournament after 2012.

Along with Bangladesh (the host) and Sri Lanka (the defending champions from the 2014 event), the tournament included India, Pakistan, and ICC associate member the United Arab Emirates, who qualified from a qualifier played from 19 to 22 February 2016.

India beat Bangladesh by 8 wickets in the final to win their sixth Asia Cup title and were unbeaten throughout the tournament.

Bhuvneshwar Kumar was added to India's squad as a replacement for Mohammed Shami after Shami failed to fully recover from a hamstring injury. Parthiv Patel was added to India's squad as a back-up for MS Dhoni, who suffered a muscle spasm. Mohammad Sami and Sharjeel Khan were added to Pakistan's squad after injuries to Babar Azam and Rumman Raees and following their performances in 2016 Pakistan Super League.Bangladesh's Mustafizur Rahman was injured during their match against Sri Lanka and was replaced for the rest of the tournament by Tamim Iqbal.

Lasith Malinga was named as Sri Lanka's captain for the tournament, but he only played in their first match. Angelo Mathews captained the side in their second and third matches while Dinesh Chandimal stood as captain in their final match.

After the Asian Cricket Council was downsized by the International Cricket Council (ICC) in April 2015, it was announced that upcoming Asia Cup events will be played on rotation basis in One Day International (ODI) and Twenty20 International (T20I) format based on respective next world events under the ICC. This means that the 2016 and 2020 events will be played using the T20I format, ahead of the 2016 and 2020 World Twenty20s, and the 2018 and 2022 events will be played in ODI format, ahead of the 2019 and 2023 World Cups respectively.

CHAPTER TWO

# Asia Cup Squad 2018

- *India national cricket team Asia Cup Squad*

The India men's national cricket team, also known as Team India and Men in Blue, represents India in men's International Cricket. It is governed by the Board of Control for Cricket in India (BCCI), and is a Full Member of the International Cricket Council (ICC) with Test, One Day International (ODI) and Twenty20 International (T20I) status.

Cricket was introduced to India by British sailors in the $18^{th}$ century, and the first cricket club was established in 1792. India's national cricket team did not play its first Test match until 25 June 1932 at Lord's, becoming the sixth team to be granted test cricket status. From 1932 India had to wait until 1952, almost 20 years for its first Test victory. In its first fifty years of international cricket, India didn't gain much success, winning only 35 of the first 196 Test matches it played. The team, however, gained strength in the 1970s with the emergence of players like Gavaskar, Viswanath, Kapil Dev, and the Indian spin quartet.

Traditionally much stronger at home than abroad, the Indian team has improved its overseas form, especially in limited-overs cricket, since the start of the $21^{st}$ century, winning Test matches in Australia, England and South Africa. It was the second cricket team to win the World Cup after West Indies. It has won the Cricket World Cup twice – in 1983 under the captaincy of Kapil Dev and in 2011 under the captaincy of MS Dhoni. After winning the 2011 World Cup, India became only the third team after West Indies and Australia to have won the World Cup more than once,and the first cricket team to win the World Cup at home.

It also won the 2007 ICC World Twenty20 and 2013 ICC Champions Trophy, under the captaincy of MS Dhoni. It was also the joint champions of 2002 ICC Champions Trophy, along with Sri Lanka. The team has also won the World Championship of Cricket in 1985 defeating Pakistan in the final. They have also won ACC Asia Cup seven times, making them one of the most successful cricket teams in both Asia and the World. They are also one of the only four teams to win all major ICC tournaments. India have also won the ICC Test Championship 5 times making them the second team to win most ICC Test Mace after Australia. They have also won the ICC ODI Championship, and the ICC T20I Championship.

The Indian cricket team has rivalries with other Test-playing nations, most notably with Pakistan, the political arch-rival of India and with Australia. However, in recent times, rivalries with nations like South Africa and England have also gained prominence.

As of 6 December 2021, India is ranked first in Tests, fourth in ODIs and second in T20Is by the ICC. Virat Kohli is the current captain of the team in Tests, while Rohit Sharma is the current captain of the team in ODIs and T20Is ,the head coach is Rahul Dravid.

India was invited to The Imperial Cricket Council in 1926, and made their debut as a Test playing nation in England in 1932, led by CK Nayudu, who was considered the best Indian batsman at the time. The one-off Test match between the two sides was played at Lord's in London. The team was not strong in their batting at this point and went on to lose by 158 runs.

India hosted its first Test series in the year 1933. England was the visiting team that played 2 Tests in Bombay (now Mumbai) and Calcutta (now Kolkata). The visitors won the series 2–0. The Indian team continued to improve throughout the 1930s and '40s but did not achieve an international victory during this period. In the early 1940s, India didn't play any Test cricket due to the Second World War. The team's first series as an independent country was in late 1947 against Sir Donald Bradman's Invincibles (a name given to the Australia national cricket team of that time). It was also the first Test series India played which was not against England. Australia won the five-match series 4–0, with Bradman tormenting the Indian bowling in his final Australian summer. India subsequently played their first Test series at home not against England, but against the West Indies in 1948. West Indies won the 5-Test series 1–0.

Queen Elizabeth II with members of the Indian team during the Indian tour of England in 1952.

India recorded their first Test victory, in their 24th match, against England at Madras in 1952. Later in the same year, they won their first Test series, which was against Pakistan.

They continued their improvement throughout the early 1950s with a series win against New Zealand in 1956. However, they did not win again in the remainder of the decade and lost badly to strong Australian and English sides. On 24 August 1959, India lost by an innings in the Test to complete the only 5–0 whitewash ever inflicted by England. The next decade saw India's reputation develop as a team with a strong record at home. They won their first Test series against England at home in 1961–62 and also won a home series against New Zealand. They managed to draw home series against Pakistan and Australia and another series against England. In this same period, India also won its first series outside the subcontinent, against New Zealand in 1967–68.

The key to India's bowling in the 1970s were the Indian spin quartet – Bishen Bedi, E.A.S. Prasanna, BS Chandrasekhar and Srinivas Venkataraghavan. This period also saw the emergence of two of India's best ever batsmen, Sunil Gavaskar and Gundappa Viswanath. Indian pitches have had the tendency to support spin and the spin quartet exploited this to create collapses in opposing batting line-ups. These players were responsible for the back-to-back series wins in 1971 in the West Indies and in England, under the captaincy of Ajit Wadekar. Gavaskar scored 774 runs in the West Indian series while Dilip Sardesai's 112 played a big part in their one Test win.

- *One-day cricket and ICC Cricket World Cup success (1970–1985)*

The advent of One Day International (ODI) cricket in 1971 created a new dimension in the cricket world. However, India was not considered strong in ODIs at this point and batsmen such as the captain Gavaskar were known for their defensive approach to batting. India began as a weak team in ODIs and did not qualify for the second round in the first two editions of the Cricket World Cup.Gavaskar infamously blocked his way to 36 not out off 174 balls against England in the first World Cup in 1975, India scored just 132 for 3 and lost by 202 runs.

In contrast, India fielded a strong team in Test matches and was particularly strong at home, where their combination of stylish batsmen and beguiling spinners were at their best. India set a then Test record in the third Test against the West Indies at Port-of-Spain in 1976, when they chased 403 to win, thanks to 112 from Viswanath. This West Indian defeat is considered to be a watershed in the history of their cricket because it led to captain Clive Lloyd dispensing with spin altogether and relying entirely on a four-man pace attack instead. In November 1976, the team established another record by scoring 524 for 9 declared against New Zealand at Kanpur without any individual batsman scoring a century. There were six fifties, the highest being 70 by Mohinder Amarnath. This innings was only the eighth instance in Test cricket where all eleven batsmen reached double figures.

During the 1980s, India developed a more attack-minded batting line-up with stroke makers such as the wristy Mohammed Azharuddin, Dilip Vengsarkar and all-rounders Kapil Dev and Ravi Shastri. India won the Cricket World Cup in 1983, defeating the favourites and the two-time defending champions West Indies in the final at Lord's, owing to a strong bowling performance. In spite of this, the team performed poorly in the Test arena, including 28 consecutive Test matches without a victory. In 1984, India won the Asia Cup and in 1985, won the World Championship of Cricket in Australia. Apart from this, India remained a weak team outside the Indian subcontinent. India's Test series victory in 1986 against England remained the last Test series win by India outside the subcontinent for the next 19 years. The 1980s saw Gavaskar and Kapil Dev (India's best all-rounder to date) at the pinnacle of their careers. Gavaskar made a Test record 34 centuries as he became the first man to reach the 10,000 run mark. Kapil Dev later became the highest wicket-taker in Test cricket with 434 wickets. The period was also marked by an unstable leadership, with Gavaskar and Kapil exchanging the captaincy several times.

The addition of Sachin Tendulkar and Anil Kumble to the national side in 1989 and 1990 further improved the team. The following year, Javagal Srinath, India's fastest bowler since Amar Singh made his debut. Despite this, during the 1990s, India did not win any of its 33 Tests outside the subcontinent while it won 17 out of its 30 Tests at home. After being eliminated by neighbours Sri Lanka on home soil at the 1996 Cricket World Cup semifinal, the team underwent a year of change as Sourav Ganguly and Rahul Dravid, later to become captains of the team, made their debut in the same Test at Lord's. Tendulkar replaced Azharuddin as captain in late 1996, but after a personal and team form slump, Tendulkar relinquished the captaincy and Azharuddin was reinstated at the beginning of 1998. With the captaincy burden removed, Tendulkar was the world's leading run-scorer in both Tests and ODIs, as India enjoyed a home Test series win over Australia, the best-ranked team in the world.

After failing to reach the semifinals at the 1999 Cricket World Cup, Tendulkar was again made captain, and had another poor run, losing 3–0 on a tour of Australia and then 2–0 at home to South Africa. Tendulkar resigned, vowing never to captain the team again. Ganguly was appointed the new captain and the team was further damaged in 2000 when former captain Azharuddin and fellow batsman Ajay Jadeja were implicated in a match-fixing scandal and given life and five years bans respectively. This period was described by the BBC as "the Indian cricket's worst hour". However, the new core – Tendulkar, Dravid, Kumble and Ganguly – swore not to let this happen to them again, and lead Indian cricket out of the dark times. And the first three put aside personal ambitions to let Ganguly lead them into a new era.

- *21st century*

- Success under Ganguly

The Indian team underwent major improvements under the captaincy of Sourav Ganguly and guidance of John Wright, India's first foreign coach. India maintained their unbeaten home record against Australia in Test series after victory in 2001. The series was famous for the Kolkata Test match, in which India became only the third team in the history of Test cricket to win a Test match after following on. Australian captain Steve Waugh labelled India as the "Final Frontier" because of his side's inability to win a Test series in India. Victory in 2001 against the Australians marked the beginning of a dream run for India under their captain Sourav Ganguly, winning Test matches in Zimbabwe, Sri Lanka, West Indies and England. The England series is also known for India's highest ODI run-chase of 325 runs at Lord's, which came in the Natwest ODI Series final against England. In the same year, India were joint-winners of the ICC Champions Trophy with Sri Lanka and then went to the 2003 Cricket World Cup in South Africa, where they reached the final, only to be beaten by Australia. The 2003–04 season also saw India play out a Test series in Australia, where they drew 1–1 with the world champions, and then win a Test and ODI series in Pakistan.

CHAPTER THREE

# Let's Know About Cricket

- *Cricket*

Cricket is a bat-and-ball game played between two teams of eleven players on a field at the centre of which is a 22-yard (20-metre) pitch with a wicket at each end, each comprising two bails balanced on three stumps. The game proceeds when a player on the fielding team, called the bowler, "bowls" (propels) the ball from one end of the pitch towards the wicket at the other end. The batting side's players score runs by striking the bowled ball with a bat and running between the wickets, while the bowling side tries to prevent this by keeping the ball within the field and getting it to either wicket, and dismiss each batter (so they are "out"). Means of dismissal include being bowled, when the ball hits the stumps and dislodges the bails, and by the fielding side either catching a hit ball before it touches the ground, or hitting a wicket with the ball before a batter can cross the crease line in front of the wicket to complete a run. When ten batters have been dismissed, the innings ends and the teams swap roles. The game is adjudicated by two umpires, aided by a third umpire and match referee in international matches.

Forms of cricket range from Twenty20, with each team batting for a single innings of 20 overs and the game generally lasting three hours, to Test matches played over five days. Traditionally cricketers play in all-white kit, but in limited overs cricket they wear club or team colours. In addition to the basic kit, some players wear protective gear to prevent injury caused by the ball, which is a hard, solid spheroid made of compressed leather with a slightly raised sewn seam enclosing a cork core layered with tightly wound string.

The earliest reference to cricket is in South East England in the mid-16$^{th}$ century. It spread globally with the expansion of the British Empire, with the first international matches in the second half of the 19$^{th}$ century. The game's governing body is the International Cricket Council (ICC), which has over 100 members, twelve of which are full members who play Test matches. The game's rules, the Laws of Cricket, are maintained by Marylebone Cricket Club (MCC) in London. The sport is followed primarily in South Asia, Australasia, the United Kingdom, southern Africa and the West Indies.Women's cricket, which is organised and played separately, has also achieved international standard. The most successful side playing international cricket is Australia, which has won seven One Day International trophies, including five World Cups, more than any other country and has been the top-rated Test side more than any other country.

- *History of cricket to 1725*

A medieval "club ball" game involving an underhand bowl towards a batter. Ball catchers are shown positioning themselves to catch a ball. Detail from the Canticles of Holy Mary, 13$^{th}$ century.

Cricket is one of many games in the "club ball" sphere that basically involve hitting a ball with a hand-held implement; others include baseball (which shares many similarities with cricket, both belonging in the more specific bat-and-ball games category), golf, hockey, tennis, squash, badminton and table tennis. In cricket's case, a key difference is the existence of a solid target structure, the wicket (originally, it is thought, a "wicket gate" through which sheep were herded), that the batter must defend. The cricket historian Harry Altham identified three "groups" of "club ball" games: the "hockey group", in which the ball is driven to and fro between two targets (the goals); the "golf group", in which the ball is driven towards an undefended target (the hole); and the "cricket group", in which "the ball is aimed at a mark (the wicket) and driven away from it".

It is generally believed that cricket originated as a children's game in the south-eastern counties of England, sometime during the medieval period.Although there are claims for prior dates, the earliest definite reference to cricket being played comes from evidence given at a court case in Guildford in January 1597 (Old Style), equating to January 1598 in the modern calendar. The case concerned ownership of a certain plot of land and the court heard the testimony of a 59-year-old coroner, John Derrick, who gave witness that.

Being a scholler in the ffree schoole of Guldeford hee and diverse of his fellows did runne and play there at creckett and other plaies.

Given Derrick's age, it was about half a century earlier when he was at school and so it is certain that cricket was being played c. 1550 by boys in Surrey. The view that it was originally a children's game is reinforced by Randle Cotgrave's 1611 English-French dictionary in which he defined the noun "crosse" as "the crooked staff wherewith boys play at cricket" and the verb form "crosser" as "to play at cricket".

One possible source for the sport's name is the Old English word "cryce" (or "cricc") meaning a crutch or staff. In Samuel Johnson's Dictionary, he derived cricket from "cryce, Saxon, a stick". In Old French, the word "criquet" seems to have meant a kind of club or stick. Given the strong medieval trade connections between south-east England and the County of Flanders when the latter belonged to the Duchy of Burgundy, the name may have been derived from the Middle Dutch (in use in Flanders at the time) "krick"(-e), meaning a stick (crook). Another possible source is the Middle Dutch word "krickstoel", meaning a long low stool used for kneeling in church and which resembled the long low wicket with two stumps used in early cricket. According to Heiner Gillmeister, a European language expert of Bonn University, "cricket" derives from the Middle Dutch phrase for hockey, met de (krik ket)sen (i.e., "with the stick chase"). Gillmeister has suggested that not only the name but also the sport itself may be of Flemish origin.

- *Growth of amateur and professional cricket in England*

Evolution of the cricket bat. The original "hockey stick" (left) evolved into the straight bat from c. 1760 when pitched delivery bowling began.

Although the main object of the game has always been to score the most runs, the early form of cricket differed from the modern game in certain key technical aspects; the North American variant of cricket known as wicket retained many of these aspects. The ball was bowled underarm by the bowler and along the ground towards a batter armed with a bat that in shape resembled a hockey stick; the batter defended a low, two-stump wicket; and runs were called notches because the scorers recorded them by notching tally sticks.

In 1611, the year Cotgrave's dictionary was published, ecclesiastical court records at Sidlesham in Sussex state that two parishioners, Bartholomew Wyatt and Richard Latter, failed to attend church on Easter Sunday because they were playing cricket. They were fined 12d each and ordered to do penance.This is the earliest mention of adult participation in cricket and it was around the same time that the earliest known organised inter-parish or village match was played – at Chevening, Kent. In 1624, a player called Jasper Vinall died after he was accidentally struck on the head during a match between two parish teams in Sussex.

Cricket remained a low-key local pursuit for much of the 17$^{th}$ century. It is known, through numerous references found in the records of ecclesiastical court cases, to have been proscribed at times by the Puritans before and during the Commonwealth. The problem was nearly always the issue of Sunday play as the Puritans considered cricket to be "profane" if played on the Sabbath, especially if large crowds or gambling were involved.

According to the social historian Derek Birley, there was a "great upsurge of sport after the Restoration" in 1660. Gambling on sport became a problem significant enough for Parliament to pass the 1664 Gambling Act, limiting stakes to £100 which was, in any case, a colossal sum exceeding the annual income of 99% of the population. Along with prizefighting, horse racing and blood sports, cricket was perceived to be a gambling sport.Rich patrons made matches for high stakes, forming teams in which they engaged the first professional players.By the end of the century, cricket had developed into a major sport that was spreading throughout England and was already being taken abroad by English mariners and colonisers – the earliest reference to cricket overseas is dated 1676. A 1697 newspaper report survives of "a great cricket match" played in Sussex "for fifty guineas apiece" – this is the earliest known contest that is generally considered a First Class match.

- The patrons, and other players from the social class known as the "gentry", began to classify themselves as "amateurs" to establish a clear distinction from the professionals, who were invariably members of the working class, even to the point of having separate changing and dining facilities. The gentry, including such high-ranking nobles as the Dukes of Richmond, exerted their honour code of noblesse oblige to claim rights of leadership in any sporting contests they took part in, especially as it was necessary for them to play alongside their "social inferiors" if they were to win their bets. In time, a perception took hold that the typical amateur who played in first-class cricket, until 1962 when amateurism was abolished, was someone with a public school education who had then gone to one of Cambridge or Oxford University – society insisted that such people were "officers and gentlemen" whose destiny was to provide leadership. In a purely financial sense, the cricketing amateur would theoretically claim expenses for playing while his professional counterpart played under contract and was paid a wage or match fee; in practice, many amateurs claimed more than actual expenditure and the derisive term "shamateur" was coined to describe the practice.

- *The Young Cricketer, 1768*

The game underwent major development in the 18th century to become England's national sport.Its success was underwritten by the twin necessities of patronage and betting. Cricket was prominent in London as early as 1707 and, in the middle years of the century, large crowds flocked to matches on the Artillery Ground in Finsbury. The single wicket form of the sport attracted huge crowds and wagers to match, its popularity peaking in the 1748 season. Bowling underwent an evolution around 1760 when bowlers began to pitch the ball instead of rolling or skimming it towards the batter. This caused a revolution in bat design because, to deal with the bouncing ball, it was necessary to introduce the modern straight bat in place of the old "hockey stick" shape.

The Hambledon Club was founded in the 1760s and, for the next twenty years until the formation of Marylebone Cricket Club (MCC) and the opening of Lord's Old Ground in 1787, Hambledon was both the game's greatest club and its focal point. MCC quickly became the sport's premier club and the custodian of the Laws of Cricket. New Laws introduced in the latter part of the 18th century included the three stump wicket and leg before wicket (lbw).

The 19th century saw underarm bowling superseded by first roundarm and then overarm bowling. Both developments were controversial.Organisation of the game at county level led to the creation of the county clubs, starting with Sussex in 1839. In December 1889, the eight leading county clubs formed the official County Championship, which began in 1890.

The most famous player of the 19th century was W. G. Grace, who started his long and influential career in 1865. It was especially during the career of Grace that the distinction between amateurs and professionals became blurred by the existence of players like him who were nominally amateur but, in terms of their financial gain, de facto professional. Grace himself was said to have been paid more money for playing cricket than any professional.

The last two decades before the First World War have been called the "Golden Age of cricket". It is a nostalgic name prompted by the collective sense of loss resulting from the war, but the period did produce some great players and memorable matches, especially as organised competition at county and Test level developed.

- *Cricket becomes an international sport*

In 1844, the first-ever international match took place between the United States and Canada. In 1859, a team of English players went to North America on the first overseas tour. Meanwhile, the British Empire had been instrumental in spreading the game overseas and by the middle of the 19th century it had become well established in Australia, the Caribbean, India, Pakistan, New Zealand, North America and South Africa.

In 1862, an English team made the first tour of Australia. The first Australian team to travel overseas consisted of Aboriginal stockmen who toured England in 1868. The first One Day International match was played on 5 January 1971 between Australia and England at the Melbourne Cricket Ground.

In 1876–77, an England team took part in what was retrospectively recognised as the first-ever Test match at the Melbourne Cricket Ground against Australia. The rivalry between England and Australia gave birth to The Ashes in 1882, and this has remained Test cricket's most famous contest. Test cricket began to expand in 1888–89 when South Africa played England.

- World cricket in the 20th century

The inter-war years were dominated by Australia's Don Bradman, statistically the greatest Test batter of all time. Test cricket continued to expand during the 20th century with the addition of the West Indies (1928), New Zealand (1930) and India (1932) before the Second World War and then Pakistan (1952), Sri Lanka (1982), Zimbabwe (1992), Bangladesh (2000), Ireland and Afghanistan (both 2018) in the post-war period. South Africa was banned from international cricket from 1970 to 1992 as part of the apartheid boycott.

- The rise of limited overs cricket

Cricket entered a new era in 1963 when English counties introduced the limited overs variant. As it was sure to produce a result, limited overs cricket was lucrative and the number of matches increased. The first Limited Overs International was played in 1971 and the governing International Cricket Council (ICC), seeing its potential, staged the first limited overs Cricket World Cup in 1975. In the 21st century, a new limited overs form, Twenty20, made an immediate impact. On 22 June 2017, Afghanistan and Ireland became the 11th and 12th ICC full members, enabling them to play Test cricket.

- A typical cricket field.

In cricket, the rules of the game are specified in a code called The Laws of Cricket (hereinafter called "the Laws") which has a global remit. There are 42 Laws (always written with a capital "L"). The earliest known version of the code was drafted in 1744 and, since 1788, it has been owned and maintained by its custodian, the Marylebone Cricket Club (MCC) in London.

- Playing area

Cricket is a bat-and-ball game played on a cricket field between two teams of eleven players each. The field is usually circular or oval in shape and the edge of the playing area is marked by a boundary, which may be a fence, part of the stands, a rope, a painted line or a combination of these; the boundary must if possible be marked along its entire length.

In the approximate centre of the field is a rectangular pitch (see image, below) on which a wooden target called a wicket is sited at each end; the wickets are placed 22 yards (20 m) apart. The pitch is a flat surface 10 feet (3.0 m) wide, with very short grass that tends to be worn away as the game progresses (cricket can also be played on artificial surfaces, notably matting). Each wicket is made of three wooden stumps topped by two bails.

- Cricket pitch and creases

As illustrated above, the pitch is marked at each end with four white painted lines: a bowling crease, a popping crease and two return creases. The three stumps are aligned centrally on the bowling crease, which is eight feet eight inches long. The popping crease is drawn four feet in front of the bowling crease and parallel to it; although it is drawn as a twelve-foot line (six feet either side of the wicket), it is, in fact, unlimited in length. The return creases are drawn at right angles to the popping crease so that they intersect the ends of the bowling crease; each return crease is drawn as an eight-foot line, so that it extends four feet behind the bowling crease, but is also, in fact, unlimited in length.

Before a match begins, the team captains (who are also players) toss a coin to decide which team will bat first and so take the first innings. Innings is the term used for each phase of play in the match.In each innings, one team bats, attempting to score runs, while the other team bowls and fields the ball, attempting to restrict the scoring and dismiss the batters. When the first innings ends, the teams change roles; there can be two to four innings depending upon the type of match. A match with four scheduled innings is played over three to five days; a match with two scheduled innings is usually completed in a single day. During an innings, all eleven members of the fielding team take the field, but usually only two members of the batting team are on the field at any given time.

The exception to this is if a batter has any type of illness or injury restricting his or her ability to run, in this case the batter is allowed a runner who can run between the wickets when the batter hits a scoring run or runs,though this does not apply in international cricket. The order of batters is usually announced just before the match, but it can be varied.

The main objective of each team is to score more runs than their opponents but, in some forms of cricket, it is also necessary to dismiss all of the opposition batters in their final innings in order to win the match, which would otherwise be drawn. If the team batting last is all out having scored fewer runs than their opponents, they are said to have "lost by n runs" (where n is the difference between the aggregate number of runs scored by the teams). If the team that bats last scores enough runs to win, it is said to have "won by n wickets", where n is the number of wickets left to fall. For example, a team that passes its opponents‘ total having lost six wickets (i.e., six of their batters have been dismissed) have won the match "by four wickets".

In a two-innings-a-side match, one team's combined first and second innings total may be less than the other side's first innings total. The team with the greater score is then said to have "won by an innings and n runs", and does not need to bat again: n is the difference between the two teams' aggregate scores. If the team batting last is all out, and both sides have scored the same number of runs, then the match is a tie; this result is quite rare in matches of two innings a side with only 62 happening in first-class matches from the earliest known instance in 1741 until January 2017. In the traditional form of the game, if the time allotted for the match expires before either side can win, then the game is declared a draw.

If the match has only a single innings per side, then a maximum number of overs applies to each innings. Such a match is called a "limited overs" or "one-day" match, and the side scoring more runs wins regardless of the number of wickets lost, so that a draw cannot occur. In some cases, ties are broken by having each team bat for a one-over innings known as a Super Over; subsequent Super Overs may be played if the first Super Over ends in a tie. If this kind of match is temporarily interrupted by bad weather, then a complex mathematical formula, known as the Duckworth–Lewis–Stern method after its developers, is often used to recalculate a new target score. A one-day match can also be declared a "no-result" if fewer than a previously agreed number of overs have been bowled by either team, in circumstances that make normal resumption of play impossible; for example, wet weather.

In all forms of cricket, the umpires can abandon the match if bad light or rain makes it impossible to continue. There have been instances of entire matches, even Test matches scheduled to be played over five days, being lost to bad weather without a ball being bowled: for example, the third Test of the 1970/71 series in Australia.

- Innings

The innings (ending with 's' in both singular and plural form) is the term used for each phase of play during a match. Depending on the type of match being played, each team has either one or two innings. Sometimes all eleven members of the batting side take a turn to bat but, for various reasons, an innings can end before they have all done so. The innings terminates if the batting team is "all out", a term defined by the Laws: "at the fall of a wicket or the retirement of a batter, further balls remain to be bowled but no further batter is available to come in". In this situation, one of the batters has not been dismissed and is termed not out; this is because he has no partners left and there must always be two active batters while the innings is in progress.

- An innings may end early while there are still two not out batters

the batting team's captain may declare the innings closed even though some of his players have not had a turn to bat: this is a tactical decision by the captain, usually because he believes his team have scored sufficient runs and need time to dismiss the opposition in their innings

the set number of overs (i.e., in a limited overs match) have been bowled

the match has ended prematurely due to bad weather or running out of time

in the final innings of the match, the batting side has reached its target and won the game.

- Overs

The Laws state that, throughout an innings, "the ball shall be bowled from each end alternately in overs of 6 balls". The name "over" came about because the umpire calls "Over!" when six balls have been bowled. At this point, another bowler is deployed at the other end, and the fielding side changes ends while the batters do not. A bowler cannot bowl two successive overs, although a bowler can (and usually does) bowl alternate overs, from the same end, for several overs which are termed a "spell". The batters do not change ends at the end of the over, and so the one who was non-striker is now the striker and vice versa. The umpires also change positions so that the one who was at "square leg" now stands behind the wicket at the non-striker's end and vice versa.

- Clothing and equipment

English cricketer W. G. Grace "taking guard" in 1883. His pads and bat are very similar to those used today. The gloves have evolved somewhat. Many modern players use more defensive equipment than were available to Grace, most notably helmets and arm guards.

The wicket-keeper (a specialised fielder behind the batter) and the batters wear protective gear because of the hardness of the ball, which can be delivered at speeds of more than 145 kilometres per hour (90 mph) and presents a major health and safety concern.

Protective clothing includes pads (designed to protect the knees and shins), batting gloves or wicket-keeper's gloves for the hands, a safety helmet for the head and a box for male players inside the trousers (to protect the crotch area). Some batters wear additional padding inside their shirts and trousers such as thigh pads, arm pads, rib protectors and shoulder pads. The only fielders allowed to wear protective gear are those in positions very close to the batter (i.e., if they are alongside or in front of him), but they cannot wear gloves or external leg guards.

Subject to certain variations, on-field clothing generally includes a collared shirt with short or long sleeves; long trousers; woolen pullover (if needed); cricket cap (for fielding) or a safety helmet; and spiked shoes or boots to increase traction. The kit is traditionally all white and this remains the case in Test and first-class cricket but, in limited overs cricket, team colours are worn instead.

- Bat and ball

Two types of cricket ball, both of the same size:

i) A used white ball. White balls are mainly used in limited overs cricket, especially in matches played at night, under floodlights (left).

ii) A used red ball. Red balls are used in Test cricket, first-class cricket and some other forms of cricket (right).

The essence of the sport is that a bowler delivers (i.e., bowls) the ball from his or her end of the pitch towards the batter who, armed with a bat, is "on strike" at the other end (see next sub-section: Basic gameplay).

The bat is made of wood, usually Salix alba (white willow), and has the shape of a blade topped by a cylindrical handle. The blade must not be more than 4.25 inches (10.8 cm) wide and the total length of the bat not more than 38 inches (97 cm). There is no standard for the weight, which is usually between 2 lb 7 oz and 3 lb (1.1 and 1.4 kg).

The ball is a hard leather-seamed spheroid, with a circumference of 9 inches (23 cm). The ball has a "seam": six rows of stitches attaching the leather shell of the ball to the string and cork interior. The seam on a new ball is prominent and helps the bowler propel it in a less predictable manner. During matches, the quality of the ball deteriorates to a point where it is no longer usable; during the course of this deterioration, its behaviour in flight will change and can influence the outcome of the match. Players will, therefore, attempt to modify the ball's behaviour by modifying its physical properties. Polishing the ball and wetting it with sweat or saliva is legal, even when the polishing is deliberately done on one side only to increase the ball's swing through the air, but the acts of rubbing other substances into the ball, scratching the surface or picking at the seam are illegal ball tampering.

- Player roles

Basic gameplay: bowler to batter

During normal play, thirteen players and two umpires are on the field. Two of the players are batters and the rest are all eleven members of the fielding team. The other nine players in the batting team are off the field in the pavilion. The image with overlay below shows what is happening when a ball is being bowled and which of the personnel are on or close to the pitch.

- Return crease

In the photo, the two batters (3 & 8; wearing yellow) have taken position at each end of the pitch (6). Three members of the fielding team (4, 10 & 11; wearing dark blue) are in shot. One of the two umpires (1; wearing white hat) is stationed behind the wicket (2) at the bowler's (4) end of the pitch. The bowler (4) is bowling the ball (5) from his end of the pitch to the batter at the other end who is called the "striker". The other batter (3) at the bowling end is called the "non-striker". The wicket-keeper (10), who is a specialist, is positioned behind the striker's wicket (9) and behind him stands one of the fielders in a position called "first slip" (11). While the bowler and the first slip are wearing conventional kit only, the two batters and the wicket-keeper are wearing protective gear including safety helmets, padded gloves and leg guards (pads).

While the umpire (1) in shot stands at the bowler's end of the pitch, his colleague stands in the outfield, usually in or near the fielding position called "square leg", so that he is in line with the popping crease (7) at the striker's end of the pitch. The bowling crease (not numbered) is the one on which the wicket is located between the return creases (12). The bowler (4) intends to hit the wicket (9) with the ball (5) or, at least, to prevent the striker (8) from scoring runs. The striker (8) intends, by using his bat, to defend his wicket and, if possible, to hit the ball away from the pitch in order to score runs.

Some players are skilled in both batting and bowling, or as either or these as well as wicket-keeping, so are termed all-rounders. Bowlers are classified according to their style, generally as fast bowlers, seam bowlers or spinners. Batters are classified according to whether they are right-handed or left-handed.

- Fielding

Of the eleven fielders, three are in shot in the image above. The other eight are elsewhere on the field, their positions determined on a tactical basis by the captain or the bowler. Fielders often change position between deliveries, again as directed by the captain or bowler.

If a fielder is injured or becomes ill during a match, a substitute is allowed to field instead of him, but the substitute cannot bowl or act as a captain, except in the case of concussion substitutes in international cricket. The substitute leaves the field when the injured player is fit to return. The Laws of Cricket were updated in 2017 to allow substitutes to act as wicket-keepers.

- Bowling and dismissal

Glenn McGrath of Australia holds the world record for most wickets in the Cricket World Cup.

Most bowlers are considered specialists in that they are selected for the team because of their skill as a bowler, although some are all-rounders and even specialist batters bowl occasionally. The specialists bowl several times during an innings but may not bowl two overs consecutively. If the captain wants a bowler to "change ends", another bowler must temporarily fill in so that the change is not immediate.

A bowler reaches his delivery stride by means of a "run-up" and an over is deemed to have begun when the bowler starts his run-up for the first delivery of that over, the ball then being "in play".

Fast bowlers, needing momentum, take a lengthy run up while bowlers with a slow delivery take no more than a couple of steps before bowling. The fastest bowlers can deliver the ball at a speed of over 145 kilometres per hour (90 mph) and they sometimes rely on sheer speed to try to defeat the batter, who is forced to react very quickly.

Other fast bowlers rely on a mixture of speed and guile by making the ball seam or swing (i.e. curve) in flight. This type of delivery can deceive a batter into miscuing his shot, for example, so that the ball just touches the edge of the bat and can then be "caught behind" by the wicket-keeper or a slip fielder. At the other end of the bowling scale is the spin bowler who bowls at a relatively slow pace and relies entirely on guile to deceive the batter. A spinner will often "buy his wicket" by "tossing one up" (in a slower, steeper parabolic path) to lure the batter into making a poor shot. The batter has to be very wary of such deliveries as they are often "flighted" or spun so that the ball will not behave quite as he expects and he could be "trapped" into getting himself out. In between the pacemen and the spinners are the medium paced seamers who rely on persistent accuracy to try to contain the rate of scoring and wear down the batter’s concentration.

There are nine ways in which a batter can be dismissed: five relatively common and four extremely rare. The common forms of dismissal are bowled, caught, leg before wicket (lbw), run out and stumped. Rare methods are hit wicket,hit the ball twice, obstructing the field and timed out. The Laws state that the fielding team, usually the bowler in practice, must appeal for a dismissal before the umpire can give his decision. If the batter is out, the umpire raises a forefinger and says "Out!"; otherwise, he will shake his head and say "Not out".There is, effectively, a tenth method of dismissal, retired out, which is not an on-field dismissal as such but rather a retrospective one for which no fielder is credited.

- Batting, runs and extras

The directions in which a right-handed batter, facing down the page, intends to send the ball when playing various cricketing shots. The diagram for a left-handed batter is a mirror image of this one.

Batters take turns to bat via a batting order which is decided beforehand by the team captain and presented to the umpires, though the order remains flexible when the captain officially nominates the team. Substitute batters are generally not allowed, except in the case of concussion substitutes in international cricket.

In order to begin batting the batter first adopts a batting stance. Standardly, this involves adopting a slight crouch with the feet pointing across the front of the wicket, looking in the direction of the bowler, and holding the bat so it passes over the feet and so its tip can rest on the ground near to the toes of the back foot.

A skilled batter can use a wide array of "shots" or "strokes" in both defensive and attacking mode. The idea is to hit the ball to the best effect with the flat surface of the bat's blade. If the ball touches the side of the bat it is called an "edge". The batter does not have to play a shot and can allow the ball to go through to the wicketkeeper. Equally, he does not have to attempt a run when he hits the ball with his bat. Batters do not always seek to hit the ball as hard as possible, and a good player can score runs just by making a deft stroke with a turn of the wrists or by simply "blocking" the ball but directing it away from fielders so that he has time to take a run. A wide variety of shots are played, the batter's repertoire including strokes named according to the style of swing and the direction aimed: e.g., "cut", "drive", "hook", "pull".

The batter on strike (i.e. the "striker") must prevent the ball hitting the wicket, and try to score runs by hitting the ball with his bat so that he and his partner have time to run from one end of the pitch to the other before the fielding side can return the ball. To register a run, both runners must touch the ground behind the popping crease with either their bats or their bodies (the batters carry their bats as they run). Each completed run increments the score of both the team and the striker.

- Sachin Tendulkar is the only player to have scored one hundred international centuries

The decision to attempt a run is ideally made by the batter who has the better view of the ball's progress, and this is communicated by calling: usually "yes", "no" or "wait". More than one run can be scored from a single hit: hits worth one to three runs are common, but the size of the field is such that it is usually difficult to run four or more. To compensate for this, hits that reach the boundary of the field are automatically awarded four runs if the ball touches the ground en route to the boundary or six runs if the ball clears the boundary without touching the ground within the boundary. In these cases the batters do not need to run. Hits for five are unusual and generally rely on the help of "overthrows" by a fielder returning the ball. If an odd number of runs is scored by the striker, the two batters have changed ends, and the one who was non-striker is now the striker. Only the striker can score individual runs, but all runs are added to the team's total.

Additional runs can be gained by the batting team as extras (called "sundries" in Australia) due to errors made by the fielding side. This is achieved in four ways: no-ball, a penalty of one extra conceded by the bowler if he breaks the rules; wide, a penalty of one extra conceded by the bowler if he bowls so that the ball is out of the batter's reach bye, an extra awarded if the batter misses the ball and it goes past the wicket-keeper and gives the batters time to run in the conventional way leg bye, as for a bye except that the ball has hit the batter's body, though not his bat. If the bowler has conceded a no-ball or a wide, his team incurs an additional penalty because that ball (i.e., delivery) has to be bowled again and hence the batting side has the opportunity to score more runs from this extra ball.

- Specialist roles

Captain (cricket) and Wicket-keeper

The captain is often the most experienced player in the team, certainly the most tactically astute, and can possess any of the main skillsets as a batter, a bowler or a wicket-keeper. Within the Laws, the captain has certain responsibilities in terms of nominating his players to the umpires before the match and ensuring that his players conduct themselves "within the spirit and traditions of the game as well as within the Laws".

The wicket-keeper (sometimes called simply the "keeper") is a specialist fielder subject to various rules within the Laws about his equipment and demeanour. He is the only member of the fielding side who can effect a stumping and is the only one permitted to wear gloves and external leg guards. Depending on their primary skills, the other ten players in the team tend to be classified as specialist batters or specialist bowlers. Generally, a team will include five or six specialist batters and four or five specialist bowlers, plus the wicket-keeper.

- Umpires and scorers

Umpire (cricket), Scoring (cricket), and Cricket statistics
An umpire signals a decision to the scorers

The game on the field is regulated by the two umpires, one of whom stands behind the wicket at the bowler's end, the other in a position called "square leg" which is about 15–20 metres away from the batter on strike and in line with the popping crease on which he is taking guard. The umpires have several responsibilities including adjudication on whether a ball has been correctly bowled (i.e., not a no-ball or a wide); when a run is scored; whether a batter is out (the fielding side must first appeal to the umpire, usually with the phrase "How's that?" or "Owzat?"); when intervals start and end; and the suitability of the pitch, field and weather for playing the game. The umpires are authorised to interrupt or even abandon a match due to circumstances likely to endanger the players, such as a damp pitch or deterioration of the light.

Off the field in televised matches, there is usually a third umpire who can make decisions on certain incidents with the aid of video evidence. The third umpire is mandatory under the playing conditions for Test and Limited Overs International matches played between two ICC full member countries. These matches also have a match referee whose job is to ensure that play is within the Laws and the spirit of the game.

The match details, including runs and dismissals, are recorded by two official scorers, one representing each team. The scorers are directed by the hand signals of an umpire . For example, the umpire raises a forefinger to signal that the batter is out (has been dismissed); he raises both arms above his head if the batter has hit the ball for six runs. The scorers are required by the Laws to record all runs scored, wickets taken and overs bowled; in practice, they also note significant amounts of additional data relating to the game.

A match's statistics are summarised on a scorecard. Prior to the popularisation of scorecards, most scoring was done by men sitting on vantage points cuttings notches on tally sticks and runs were originally called notches.According to Rowland Bowen, the earliest known scorecard templates were introduced in 1776 by T. Pratt of Sevenoaks and soon came into general use.It is believed that scorecards were printed and sold at Lord's for the first time in 1846.

- *thank you for buy & read this book*

have a great day of your
from : Mr Vivek Kumar Pandey

9 798885 306782

Printed by Libri Plureos GmbH in Hamburg,
Germany